I0477755

INVESTING FOR RETIREMENT

INVESTMENT SERIES
CONCISE READS™

PETER OLIVER

INVESTING FOR RETIREMENT
Copyright © 2019 by Concise Reads™

CONTENTS

PREFACE

I gnorance is bliss--that is unless we're talking about personally financing our retirement. By all accounts, my childhood and early adulthood were blessed. Both my parents worked 70-80 hour weeks and provided every privilege I could ask for. My parents drove the same old car and wore the same clothes for decades, foregoing any luxuries so that they could afford my education. I excelled in math and science, played sports, learned multiple languages, travelled the world, and went to the best schools. With a good head on my shoulders and an inherited strong work ethic, I was destined to make a salary reserved for the 1%. Why would I ever consider planning for retirement? After all, my own father told me he never plans on retiring unless he is wheeled from his job site to the grave. Admirable, but unlike my grandparents and great grandparents who passed away while they were still working, today--we live much longer than our bodies and minds are capable of staying competitive in

1

the labor force.

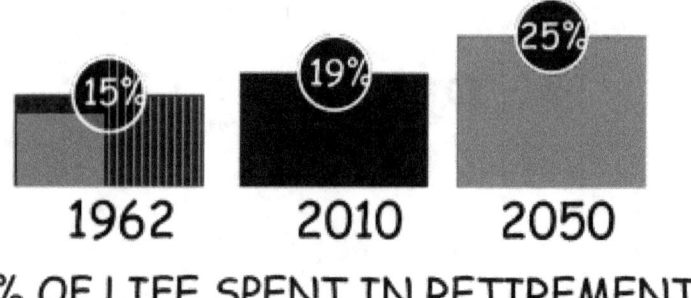

% OF LIFE SPENT IN RETIREMENT

At some point, even if we don't want to,
we will be forced to retire.

My wakeup call came in 2008. I had completed one graduate degree and was pursuing a second while continuing to work in my off hours. I worked 80 hours a week then and still continue to do so today. I was focused on maximizing my salary without thinking about maximizing my time in the future which becomes more valuable the older you get. It was then that I read Rich Dad Poor Dad which didn't give me much guidance except that it changed my **perspective** on how I think about the value of time. The premise of the book is that the general population is working for the next paycheck, week in and week out, constantly working towards a bigger paycheck until they reach the government identified retirement age. The book challenges us to think how we could stop working for money and instead have money work for us. The book similar to a lot of other self-help books is just a teaser to get the readers to enroll in follow up courses, seminars, and other more expensive learning formats. I never paid for those, nor cared for them. I focused my energies on this idea that I could make money work for me so that my retirement is secure, and my family is secure for decades even after I'm gone.

The lesson I learned with regards to personally financing my retirement is that I needed to take a more active role in securing mine and my family's future. In 2008, I could see that the Bull Run after the dot com bubble was nearing its end. In January of 2008, the S&P 500 index dropped by 6%. The last time it had that significant of a decline was in 1990, and this is after a gain of 1.5% in January of 2007 and 2.65% in January of 2006. I was extremely pre-occupied with my career at the time, but assumed the professionals handling my retirement accounts could see the warning signs. They may have, but they <u>did not sell</u>. There is an inherent problem with managers of retirement accounts. They <u>do not sell</u>. If they liquidate stocks to cash to wait out the recession which happens after every bull run, then they risk having clients pulling their money out which reduces the total assets under management, and guess what? Reduces their take home salary because they get paid on a percentage of the total assets under management. By the end of 2009, my entire retirement portfolio had lost 40% of its value, something that took me several years to save. You can imagine how frustrated I was with fund managers thinking they can beat the stock market during a recession. If it lasts 6 months or 18 months they will continue to trade my money as long as they have a job to go to every morning. I had said enough is enough with these professionals losing my hard earned money. After all, what's the point of working so hard if I lose my savings?

I decided to take a more active role when it comes to my retirement security. The first thing I did was put $2000 in a trading account with a discount brokerage firm and practiced, practiced, practiced. I turned that $2000 into $48,000 then lost most of it and started again. The second time around, I started reading books, newspapers, anything I could get my hands on. I also talked to my colleagues about each other's retirement portfolio. If you are close enough, people in general are very happy to compare notes and learn something new when it comes to securing their retirement. It's not a competition!

I slowly started to build an educational foundation so that I don't end up on the losing side of my advisor's financial advice. Today, I trade much less often and with much higher returns. This first guide in the series will not teach you to trade. The second guide will. However, this guide will teach you how to think about personally financing your retirement and what you need to know to get a better handle on money you've earned through your blood, sweat, and tears--hopefully no tears were shed in the workplace. In August 2018 I knew the Bull Run was as good as done, and I asked my old firm to liquidate my retirement account and forward it into an IRA account that I control in cash. After some paperwork and a painful 6 weeks of waiting, my retirement account was in cash, in my account, and under my control by September 2018. I then disappointingly saw how fund managers continued to send email newsletters stating that the worst is over, that there is potential for another run up, and any garbage that would have people keep their money trading during a recession. October, November, December came and went and I started hearing how people lost 40-50% of their retirement accounts and now it's too late to liquidate because their managers told them they would miss the returns of a subsequent rise in stock prices. There will be a subsequent run up, also known as a bear trap in the first months of 2019 but the long term bull trend is reversing.

To put it in perspective, if we had just a little bit of education on investing and retirement planning and decided to move our money out of stocks and into cash or government backed and inflation adjusted bonds, then our annual compounding return would be 15% between 2003 and 2017.

INTRODUCTION

I nvesting is not complicated at all, but the vast majority of us don't understand investing. That is why some of the highest paid professions-- and we're talking about comfortable 6 figure salaries--are ones where professionals take a commission for investing your money!

Over the years I've worked with a lot of these professionals, some ok, some barely ok. One thing they had in common is that they were very confident. Confident enough to make me feel confident that my money was in good hands. Taken to the dark extreme, the con man is essentially a confidence man--someone who gives you confidence in their abilities. This is not to say that all finance professionals are con men, but I rather believe in statistics. The statistics tell us that venture capitalists who invest other people's money and take a commission (a 2% management fee and a 20% profit sharing fee also known as carry) can't beat the returns from just investing in the market. Hedge funds similarly make the hedge fund manager extremely rich but compared to the market they are poor performers. You might hear a new hedge fund manager quote you 30% returns in the past three years of a bull cycle, but give them enough time (and enough statistical data points) and guess what? They still underperform the market. When the stock market was crashing in 2018, wealth managers (another group of bankers who take a commission for handling rich people's money) sent out emails saying that there is potential for the market to turn around soon and they are optimistic! They also underperformed.

Why do I mention all this? Because I want to empower you and share the perspective that unless you find an anomaly (someone who is more than 2 standard deviations from the average performers), then you are fully capable and qualified to take a more active role in the decision making process when it comes to YOUR hard earned cash.

This series will cover the basics with some of my personal anecdotes. The goal is not to have you pass any of the 'series' exams for a financial advisor (which I actually took back when I was contemplating becoming a financial advisor) but rather to give you the tools and confidence that all the information you need to become capable and knowledgeable is available should you choose to learn it.

WHY INVEST?

Investing wisely is a way for your money to work hard for you. Rich Dad taught us that we need our money working for us so that one day we don't have to work for our money. If it only takes a few hours to make some smart choices with the potential to gain a 10 or 20% return, then you should think of that return as how many days you DIDN'T work for that return. For example let's say you have 10 years of income saved up which after taxes and expenses is equivalent to 5 years of income. Then a 20% return on your investment is the same thing as working 9 to 5 (or longer) for an entire year! I want you to think of it that way.

The second take home I want you to always remember is the power of compounding. If you have a return of 20% year after year for 5 years, does that mean you made back 5 years' worth of hard work? Not exactly. If you reinvested your earnings, and let's assume this is a retirement account without any taxes paid, then your return after 5 years is 1.2*1.2*1.2*1.2*1.2 OR 1.2^5. If you plug that into your calculator or just type 1.2^5 into the google search bar you get 2.5 or 250%! That's 12.5 years of hard labor that you would have had to work for compared to what we thought would be just 5 years. That's the power of compounding! Of course I simplified it by not including taxes and not taking into account the possibility of going from a bull market to a bear market, but we'll cover those later in this guide.

A great example of compounding is if you held on to APPLE stock from 1980 for the next 35-40 years (that's a long time!), you would end up with a tremendous gain of 242.6 times your original investment! However, if we take that gain and break it up over the 37 years it took to achieve it, we find that annual returns were 16% which is still pretty good but it tempers the fear of missing out and finding that ONE stock that will make you a millionaire in 40 years. To do the same arithmetic we just did simply plug in (242.6)^1/37 into the google search bar and you'll get 1.16 which is a 16% year on year growth. In 1980, betting on Apple was a gamble unless you really understood the industry APPLE was in. If you're gambling, then do so with a small amount that you are willing to lose because you don't have the industry knowledge to strengthen the confidence behind your bet.

Peter Oliver

Having an understanding of compounding and that investing could help move your family to a better financial position, let's now look at what investment choices are available. We can invest in stocks of public companies, into bonds (whether corporate or government), Exchange Traded Funds (or ETFs), their more expensive mutual funds, Indices which mirror the market and are traded just like stocks, startups (if you are an accredited investor), real estate (rehab or rental properties), and of course you could invest into your own small business.

There is no right or wrong investment, but it's important to follow two rules:

1. Only invest in what you know. This is Warren Buffet's number one rule.
2. Don't diversify, but don't put all your eggs in one type of investment either.

The second point alludes to something known as asset classes. Assets can have different classes such as stocks, bonds, real estate, startups, etc. Robert Kiyosaki puts his money in real estate, in his business, and a much smaller portion in stocks. I put some of my money in real estate, small businesses, and seed or series A startups while the bulk is in ETFs and a smaller portion reserved for small cap technology stocks in an industry that I am an expert in and can tell the difference between a company that will succeed and one that won't. If the real estate market goes belly up, hopefully I would have seen that coming (with higher interest rates, and higher credit defaults) but if I didn't, then I'm not in the dog house and I might end the year with a profit because I've diversified into different asset classes.

In this guide we will cover the basics of investing, how you should think about retirement, bonds & fixed income, Mutual funds & ETFs, Stocks, Real Estate, Commodities, Options & Futures, and Alternative Investments. There is a lot to cover, and I'm excited you're taking this first step. This first guide will dig deeper into ETFs as that is a good starting point in the world of investing. The next guide in the series will dig deeper into what's known as **technical trading** for stocks. Subsequent guides in the series will mirror the learning interests of our online community at https://www.concisereads.com.

BEWARE OF GET RICH SEMINARS

When I read Robert Kiyosaki's original book *Rich Dad Poor Dad,* I had a shift in perspective when it comes to the topic of retirement. Robert had multiple failed businesses before he finally decided to take his own advice more seriously with a focus on retirement and he was able to retire about 10-11 years later. His insights about the diminishing value (read: real economic value) of a college education, that your personal home is a liability, and that lowering your tax burden should be one of your biggest methods of increasing your savings are all brilliant. Insights aside, the real meat of applying these insights is left to the entrepreneurial reader which is what I was more than a decade ago. Of course to learn the actual 'how-to' you'd have to sign up for his seminars to learn more.

Let's understand a little about the rise of Robert Kiyosaki. Robert was honorably discharged from the Marine Corps in 1974, and started a company in 1977 called Rippers that brought to market the first nylon and Velcro surfer wallet. By all accounts, it was a moment of ingenuity because there was a need in the market and Velcro technology was already developed. Unfortunately, he didn't bother thinking about protecting his intellectual property and soon enough there were several copy cats with better marketing skills and his company went bankrupt. He then started a merchandising retail business selling branded t-shirts, hats, bags, etc for popular rock bands. That company also went bankrupt. He then went on to launch Cashflow Technologies which sold the Rich Dad (books & seminars) and the Cashflow brand (books and board games). The money from this last business, he turned into a fortune by investing in real estate, the stock market, and private oil wells. By his account, he wasn't a very good writer and his books were mainly written by others. In more recent news, he had partnered with a company that sold 'get rich quick' seminars using his name and image. In 2010, and again more recently in the news, one such company that partnered with him was using predatory practices to rip people from their hard earned money such as convincing them to apply for a $100,000 credit line and spend $40,000 on the final and more expensive seminar in the series. Any people who objected were kicked out of the program to prevent them from affecting the others who were already hooked. Caught by media backlash, Robert soon distanced himself from them. Now, while I appreciate the initial perspective changing insights in Rich Dad Poor Dad, the get rich seminars I thought, would not be something Robert would have gotten involved with from the start. That could have been the plan all along, but no one knows for sure.

I've attended similar seminars in the past and was disgusted by how they use behavioral psychology to weed out the non-believers and force the believers to pay fees up to $50,000 just to learn the 'secret' to getting rich. I even saw a young millennial on Youtube talk about how the seminar taught him that you can have all the hope in the world to become rich but unless you take 'action' you will never find out if you can succeed. By advocating 'action' the seminar got the participants to spend more money on their products. The millennial on Youtube was so proud of himself for taking 'action' and oblivious to how motivation psychology works in sales. Because I was annoyed by these in the past but had no medium to educate others, I'd like to spend 5-10 minutes to quickly do so now.

These companies spend a lot of money on advertisements and email spam. They usually recruit a celebrity to put on their advertisements. This celebrity is someone who made a lot of money doing something and they promise that <u>you too</u> can become rich. They then tell you that they are holding FREE seminars in your city. If you sign up, not only will you get to hear transformational advice but you will be eligible to walk away with several books, a software, something worth $100 in value for FREE. You sign up and go to these seminars none the wiser except for hope that you will somehow outperform every other person who receives the <u>same information</u>.

My mentee, Richard went to a seminar by Than Merrill that promised to teach him how to make a lot of money in real estate. What he told me was not surprising. He signed up for the FREE seminar. The people who attended these seminars were poor or lower middle class. They looked like people who should not be spending their hard earned money on get rich seminars. The seminar was targeted to them. The sales people knew the doubters would not cough up any money so the seminar was not intended for *them*. At the seminar, Richard was given informational material with the picture of the celebrity and testimonials on how much money other students made. I wondered what percentage of ALL students these success stories represented. That statistic is never given out. It's never the case that they would say 99% of all the people who paid for the seminar made a million dollars. It's always that John, and Bob, and Sally all became rich. Who the heck are John, Bob, and Sally? To Richard's disappointment, the celebrity did not attend the local free seminar. A 'hard sell' salesman came up and talked very confidently and with authority. He said that it's hard to make money but if the audience really commits, if they follow the advice, and take 'action' they too can become rich. Then he went into describing what an expert he was. This is known as <u>establishing credibility</u> which we talked about in the Concise Reads guide on effective communication (in the management series). Of course, I never understood why an expert investor would be working as a full time salesperson and I rhetorically asked Richard that. That aside, Richard said the salesperson did something that I've seen done several times before in these seminars. He forced a lot of audience participation. This is known as 'buy-in' and in the Concise Reads effective communication guide, I mention that that is very important to create an **engaged** audience. An engaged audience is more likely to buy, believe, or agree with what it is you are selling.

The salesperson got people to tell their stories, and even made an obvious statement saying 'Folks, do we make money when we BUY a house or when we SELL a house'. The group was not sure, and he started calling on different people until finally he revealed that we make money when we BUY a house. My mind was blown. Not really. Why would anyone buy an overpriced house they can't sell? The group was astonished at this insight, and he said this is just a taste of what they will learn in the follow up seminars. He then asked the group to use the pen and paper that was given to them and write down some of the 'facts' he made. Richard could see that people all around him were actually writing down what he told them to write down. Then he went through a hypothetical example of a purchase and sale one student made and again asked the audience to calculate how much profit she made. By the time the seminar was over, he said the same thing that all the salespeople say after a FREE seminar. That is, that no one can really learn how to become rich in one seminar BUT if they pay $1000 dollars for the follow up 3-day seminar they will get import-ant tools they need to succeed. What he didn't say is that by the end of the 3-day seminar, the most motivated students (read gullible) are approached by confident salespeople to convince them to enroll in the longer 1 week seminar in which the celebrity himself will be teaching them for a mere $10,000-$50,000. Before the seminar finished, he said that normally the 3-day seminar costs $1000 but if Rich-ard and the audience were to pay TODAY he'll give them a discounted rate of $300 but only if they pay today. To Richard's surprise, the majority of the room lined up to pay for the 3-day seminar.

This process of getting you to commit to something for FREE, creating an engaged audience, getting you to make another small commitment for a 3-day seminar, and then again getting you to commit to a more expensive seminar is morally unethical, at least in my opinion. There is no get rich quick scheme, and there is no way successful investors would be selling their 'secret' formula. There is only sound financial knowledge and it should never cost more than a few dollars.

Robert Kiyosaki is not the only celebrity to have partnered with get rich seminars or cleverly categorized as 'event organizers'. Believe it or not, many of the investors from the popular Shark Tank show have done the same thing. I once saw an advertisement on LinkedIn that a multi-millionaire celebrity will be giving out financial advice. The company advertisement was like any get rich seminar. In fact to see for yourself, just type 'get rich seminar' and a millionaire celebrity's name and you'll see what I'm referencing. My journey down this rabbit hole, for research purposes, promised me free books and DVDs on the secrets of getting rich and making money in any situation. When I visited the website of the event organizers, it looked typical of the get rich seminars. There were promises of life changing information followed by the promise of advice from a millionaire celebrity, followed by free books and gifts just for signing up for the FREE event. I then read the disclaimers, the terms & conditions, and the privacy statements. The disclaimers for those who take the time to read them would shock you. There is a disclaimer that testimonials were handpicked based on overall satisfaction with the course. Another that by signing up you give them the right to sell your data. Another disclaimer that they install cookies on your browsers to get data on all the sites you visited outside of their site regardless if you have a 'Do Not Track' or DNT option activated in your browser. They sell that data as well. Lastly, a tiny disclaimer that the celebrity may or may not make an appearance in the actual seminar.

Mr. Wonderful' or Kevin O'Leary is partnered with Wealth Retreat Events which also owns the sharkevent.com website and whose marketing is conducted by another company called response.com. The same disclaimers on response.com can also be found on the OnWealthEvent.com website which advertises advice from Robert Herjavec, another Shark Tank Millionaire, and on prosperlive.com.

Look, I can't make the case whether $50,000 advice makes sense for you. I can only share first-hand experience from my mentee, Richard, and warnings from the Better Business Bureau which is a non-profit organization that catalogs all complaints against a business entity, displays them on their website, rates the business from F to A, and issues articles to warn the public. Let's look at what they have to say in one instance.

The Better Business Bureau alerted the public that a Utah based company called Zurixx, LLC was promoting FREE tickets to a talk by another Shark Tank millionaire, Daymond John. Zurixx has received hundreds of complaints and is poorly rated by the BBB. Here is what the Better Business Bureau (bbb.org) reported as complaints:

1. Complainants tell BBB they originally were attracted to the seminars by free tickets.
2. The mailer touts free gifts, including cash, gift cards and smartwatches, being given away throughout the day. The mailer also includes a letter from John in it. "This will be a life-changing event!" John writes in bold lettering.
3. They were then asked to pay $1,997 to attend a three-day event.
4. Consumers said while they attended the three-day event they were asked to spend up to $50,000 for additional packages.
5. Previous BBB investigations into similar seminars have found the celebrities endorsing the event rarely appear.
6. In addition to the John programs, Zurixx also has used the names Advanced Financial Training, Advanced Real Estate Education, Flipping Formula Education, Premium Financial Training, Shark Academy, Success Path Education, SuccessPath and USA Loan Processing.

These get rich seminars are not a new invention

and despite likely having very poor outcomes for the majority of students (never something that is reported aside from a handful of positive testimonials), millions of dollars are spent on them every year---and it is completely legal! As long as they put a disclaimer that nothing they say is financial advice, the Securities and Exchange Commission (SEC) are happy. As long as they say that results vary, and some people might make money and others might not, then the FTC's Bureau of Consumer Protection is happy because it's not deemed 'deceptive' advertising. What happens if a company receives a lot of bad media press from consumers who complain that they felt taken advantage of? Well, what often happens is the company that is being run as an LLC would shut down its business, and the same owners would set up a new LLC with a brand new name and clear reputation. This is a typical practice in business and in relation to investing, something that is quite common practice in the mutual fund world. Though in the world of investing specifically, a poorly performing fund is closed down, a new fund with the same fund manager is opened up, and if it has even marginal positive returns in the next few months, it is heavily marketed to consumers until it eventually underperforms and is also shut down.

HOW TO
THINK ABOUT
RETIREMENT

15% of Americans Aged 60+ Have No Retirement Saving

Percentage of Americans who have no retirement saving/pension, by age group

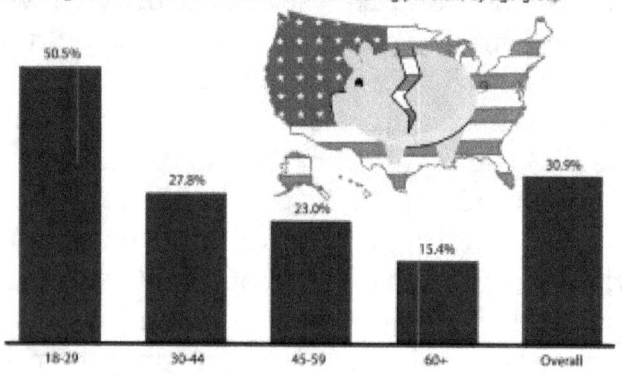

50.5%
27.8%
23.0%
15.4%
30.9%

18-29   30-44   45-59   60+   Overall

Source: Federal Reserve

I deally you should have started planning for retirement in your 20s because of the power of compound interest. An account that gains a measly 2% above inflation over 10 years generates $(1.02)\wedge10$ or 22% return. The same account over 40 years generates $(1.02)\wedge40$ or 121%. Having said that, we live a very long time with a third of our life in formal education, a third of our life working, and another third in retirement. How well we manage out retirement fund is imperative for our survival.

The first step to take when it comes to thinking about retirement is to calculate all your current expenses. This includes the health insurance that is partially or fully paid for by your employer. As an example, let's assume all your expenses are $50,000 per year. That is, you need to spend $50,000 a year just to maintain your lifestyle. Will that be enough in retirement? No. Our health insurance premiums and medical expenses (think prescriptions) will increase as we get older. We also have to take into account taxes. $50,000 is what I want to spend at age 70.5 years old but I would need an income of 50,000/0.7 or $71,428 per year from my retirement fund assuming total taxes of 30%. We also have to take into account inflation! I may be spending $50,000 per year at age 70.5 years old but by the time my little old body reaches 100 years old, with a conservative inflation rate of 2% per year I would be spending $121,363 per year!

To keep things simple, let's assume a tax rate of 30% and inflation of 2%, and let's assume that our expenses will be able to cover an increase in health insurance premiums, and we'll pay for cheaper generic drugs in our old age. How much TOTAL will we need in retirement?

Financial advisors would say you should have enough for 30 years of retirement. Sound advice, because most of us will expire before then. However, I have a healthy egotistical viewpoint that I will outlive my classmate bully Jimmy, and reach 100 years old. In that case, I would follow my mother's sage advice.

Never spend your principal.

The principal must be maintained in the event of catastrophe. The principal is my rainy day fund. That means I would need enough of a retirement fund to be able to pay my expenses from the income generated on the principle. In fact, I want only a portion of that income to go to expenses, and the rest to go back and increase the principal. The stock market as a whole averages 7% returns per year. If we assume a less conservative inflation rate of 3%, then I can borrow 4% of the principle and my principle will grow at the same rate of inflation. I would go a step further and say I should use only 2-3% of my principle assuming an average return of 7%. If I'm only using 2-3% of my principle, then I should be financially secure even if I live to 120 years old. If my expenses are $50,000 and taxes are 30%, then that 2-3% will need to account for $71,428 pre-tax income. That means my principle must be $71,428/0.03 = $2,380,933!

SOCIAL SECURITY

F ortunately, I can save you a heart attack by reminding you that additional sources of income in retirement come in the form of employee pension plans and social security. Let's assume this additional income is $21,428 per year. Then your principal for your retirement fund needs to be $50,000/0.03 = 1,666,666. This is still a lot, but much lower than the $2.3 million prior to taking into account social security and pension benefits. In 2018, the maximum social security monthly check was about $2700 and that's if your income hit the maximum taxable income for each of the last 35 years (or the 35 years with the highest income if you worked for longer than that). The 2018 social security income cap is $128,400 and the 2019 cap is $132,900.

If you were born after 1960, then normal retirement age is 67 but you can begin claiming social security at age 62. That's not my plan. Why? Because if you decide to pick up social security at age 62 years old, your monthly income check will be reduced to 70% of the normal retirement age benefit for the rest of your life. Even if you pick the check at age 65 years old just two years prior to 67, you will only get 86.7% of the full retirement benefit! Now, if you can delay receiving a social security check then do it. In 2017, if you deferred retirement for 1 year to age 68, then you would receive an additional 8% per year of deferment for the rest of your life. So if you defer for 3 years, you would get 1.08*1.08*1.08= almost 26% increase in your monthly social security check. 8% is better than the average return in the stock market, so again IF you can--defer receiving social security retirement benefits. Of course, the caveat is that there is no guarantee if you defer retirement in 2019, there is no chance the social security administration will go bankrupt in 2020. Unlikely, but that is a fear every person who is close to retirement has when they are depending on social security for their expenses because their retirement fund is not large enough.

What happens if you are nearing retirement and you don't have enough money in your retirement fund? The answer for those who started saving a little late is simple -- decrease your expenses and delay retirement. Mr. Money Mustache, or Peter Adeney's story is helpful though not entirely practical but it is a good example to use when talking about expenses. Peter and his ex-wife both software engineers made about $70,000 a year each. After saving about $600,000 they retired. Today, Peter runs a successful blog and financial advice business that brings in $400,000 or more per year. But let's look at the numbers. He retired with $600,000 and used the 4% rule, or the belief that if you withdraw 4% of the principle then the principle should be able to last forever regardless of inflation. That means his annual income in retirement would be $24,000 prior to taxes. His investments include simple investments in indices or ETFs which we'll talk about next, and that was enough for him to retire at 30. In fact, Mr. Mustache publicly explains that his annual expenses are $10,000 or less and his blog shows you how to pinch here and there. The lesson is not to make your own kombucha at home, or ride a bike at age 70 to cut costs. The lesson is that your only choice to be able to retire with a less than desired retirement fund is to SIGNIFICANTLY CUT your expenses. I personally really enjoy driving a car and taking a vacation every once in a while to encounter new cultures and traditions. That's why I'm working hard and saving more to be able to afford those things in retirement and still not touch my principal.

I think this was a very important discussion to build a framework for how you should think of your retirement fund. I do need to state something obvious. Let's say your fund returned 5% and inflation was 3% for a particular year. You should pay attention to these metrics, don't just borrow the same dollar amount every year. To keep from touching the principal AND keeping up with inflation, then we are left with 2% of the principle. Ideally, you would cut down on some of the luxuries for that year until you have a better return the following year. My 3% rule instead of the 4% rule is on purpose to encourage myself to strive to INCREASE my principle above the rate of inflation by SAVING more instead of taking riskier investments. You might be thinking if the principle could last forever if you take out the rest of the income after saving for inflation, why should you save even more? Well, personally I want to be able to leave something behind for my loved ones.

ASSET
ALLOCATION

Asset allocation is a broad term referencing the allocation of your retirement fund to different assets from real estate, stocks, bonds, and even annuities. To begin with, let's talk about your employer retirement accounts. This is the 401K or 401b (if you work for a non-profit). Your employer offers to match a certain percentage of your income as an employee benefit/perk. Take them on their offer. You will likely never achieve 100% returns anywhere else. If your employer offers to match 5% of your salary to fund your retirement account, then allocate 5% of your income to the retirement fund.

Next, you have the option of putting money away into a Roth 401k. The Roth is post-tax funds whose earnings can continue to be invested (and not taxed as income) for the rest of your life. You are allowed to begin withdrawing funds at the age of 59.5 years old from a Roth account. If you withdraw earlier, you'll face a 10% penalty. The Roth 401k is limited to a maximum contribution of $18,500 in 2018 ($19,000 in 2019 plus $6000 for employees older than 50 years old). This maximum limit applies to the combined value of the Roth 401k and the pre-tax IRA.

> IRAs and 401ks are not investments. They are tax-deferred investment accounts.

The IRA is an individual (personal) retirement account offered by any brokerage firm including discount brokerage firms like Fidelity. The 401k and 401b is offered by your employer and have limited investment choices. In fact, one of my mentees called me up because his company's 401k does not offer an inverse ETF which is an exchange traded fund that is inversely correlated with a market index or another ETF. That means if the stock market goes down (which he expects it to) then the inverse ETF will go up. This is the problem with the 401k and 401b, not only do they have limited funds to choose from, you don't have the choice to sell the invested stocks whenever you want. There is a delayed quarterly or annual rebalancing when you are allowed to change the options you chose from riskier investments to safer ones. On the other hand, an IRA gives you a lot more choice AND with some brokerage, the ability to buy and sell any stock you want with your retirement fund almost instantaneously. Don't invest in single stocks. We'll talk about investing next. For now understand that once you leave your employer, it is good practice to rollover your 401 retirement account to an IRA with the brokerage firm of your choosing though Vanguard and Fidelity are good options because they offer what's known as commission free funds to invest your retirement funds into. You can also fund your own Roth IRA account or rollover a Roth 401k account to Roth IRA (i.e. your own individual retirement account). Note however, that a Roth IRA has a maximum contribution of $6,000 in 2019 (plus an additional $1000 for employees 50 years old or older). Common sense would say to maximize the Roth 401k and only rollover the account after you leave your current company. This is especially important to do before the age of 70.5 years because with a Roth 401k you are required to start taking distributions (withdrawals) at that age whereas with a Roth IRA you do not have any such requirement and you can let the principle grow <u>tax free</u>.

The reason I personally maximized my investments in my employer's Roth 401k or traditional 401k and only AFTER I left my employer did I rollover that amount into my personal IRA account is because of restrictions with the tax law. If I was to fund my IRA account directly, I am limited to $6000 total for both a traditional and a Roth IRA. On the other hand contribution limits for a 401k is $18,500 (in 2018) if you are under 50 years old and $24,500 if you are 50 or older. The total contribution is shared with a Roth 401k. This means you can contribute up to the maximum in the 401k, the Roth 401k, or both.

It is very important to be aware of any vesting schedule for your employer contribution. Some employers entice new employees by offering to match up to 5% or 10% of their salaries in contributions to their 401k. However, in the fine print it may state that these contributions are vested over a number of years. In other words, the company could allow you to claim the 20% of the employer contributions each year over the next 5 years, or 100% ONLY after working with them for 3 years. Legally, employers can set up a vesting schedule that is as long as 6 years, but more than half of employers vest employer contributions to a 401k immediately. Just be wary of your situation before leaving your employer and rolling over your 401k.

There's another reason why I personally maximize my 401k accounts before rolling them over to my IRA account every year. The reason is because I don't qualify to contribute directly to my IRA account. Hopefully this will apply to you as well in the near future if it doesn't already! If you make more than $135,000 (in 2018) or $137,000 (in 2019) you are not allowed to contribute to a Roth IRA. If you make more than $63,000 (in 2018) or

$64,000(in 2019) then you can't deduct pre-tax dollars above that limit. Consequently, albeit delayed by a year, I get to fund my IRA account with $18,500 of my own money AND a little bit more from my employer's contribution (which does not count toward the total contribution limit). This is close to $30k every year instead of the $5,500 limit and I get to control my retirement portfolio through my online discount brokerage firm. Consult with a tax accountant for formal advice, but this is my plan with an eye on the long-term to grow my retirement portfolio tax-free long after I reach 59.5 years old. Remember, IRAs do not have a required distribution at age 70, which means I can keep growing my account well past 70 years old, taking out only what I need to survive, and leaving the rest for my family after I'm gone.

Marriage helps reduce taxes when filing jointly because you get to fall into a lower tax bracket and get to have higher income limits before not being able to contribute to your IRA accounts. Interestingly, our **tax brackets** are <u>more modern</u> than the income limits for **IRA contributions**. You might wonder where I'm going with this. Amusingly, I think you'll find it interesting as well. The income limits for IRA contribution are <u>less than</u> twice as much for joint filers than for single filers. For example a single filer has an income limit of $63,000 (in 2018), while married couples filing jointly have an income limit of $101,000. On the other hand the maximum limit for taxable income to remain in the 22% tax bracket (for 2018) is $82,500 for single filers and $165,000 for married couples filing jointly. This means if you and your spouse have an <u>equal</u> salary, then filing jointly will not affect your tax bracket when compared to filing as single, and will have a negative effect on your eligibility for IRA contributions when compared to filing as single. Note however, that if you each are making $300,000 or more, you'll fall in a lower tax bracket if you file separately rather than jointly. If you are making that much, then you likely already know that. One of the first discussions a newly married couple should have, is with their tax accountant to maximize how much money they get to keep and how much Uncle Sam gets when filing jointly or separately. Every situation is different, but over the long term, learning what the benefits and disadvantages are for the simple question of filing jointly or separately is an important one to tackle before or as soon as you are married for better or worse. Hopefully better.

Now that we've settled how to think about retirement accounts, next up is a short discussion on Annuities as an asset class. Annuities are sold by private insurance companies. If you pay them a large principal, they guarantee to pay you either a <u>fixed</u> payment of 4.5% for example or a <u>variable</u> payment based on the fund's performance. The insurance company takes your money, then invests it in stocks and bonds, makes a return, and gives you a smaller return. The reason annuities are attractive is because of this 'guarantee' of payment which can be comforting. For example, if you have $3 million in your retirement fund but know that you'll need $50,000 per year for expenses, then you would pay for a fixed 4.5% annuity with a premium of $1.11 million upfront. That way regardless of what happens to the rest of your principle, you are 'guaranteed' $50,000 a year in income as long as the insurance company does not go bankrupt during your lifespan and you don't expire early. If you expire a year after shelling out that premium, then the insurance company <u>gets to keep the money</u> and your heirs don't have a claim to it. How much of an insurance company's revenue comes from people dying off early or from sound investment decisions is <u>unknown</u>. The important point is that if you don't have an appetite for risky investments or being involved with investing your retirement fund, this may be an option for you. Consult with a financial advisor to get more information, and think critically if this is the best option for your circumstances. You are the ultimate decider.

The simplest asset allocation is between stocks and bonds. Stocks are risky investments with an average return of 7% with some stocks such as technology stocks (Nasdaq QQQ) having **20-30% returns** only when the market is in a bull market (the opposite of 2008). The older you are, or I should say, the closer you are to retirement the more likely you would care about securing your principal. In other words, your investment portfolio allocation between stocks and bonds would skew in favor of bonds as they are less risky (and therefore have smaller returns). That is not to say that all 'old' people should invest solely in bonds. This depends on your risk tolerance, and your risk tolerance depends on how big your retirement fund is and your personal preference. If you can safely survive in retirement by using only 1% or 0.5% of your principal, then you risk losing 2-2.5% of your principle. In other words, if we assume that investing in stocks could risk you losing 20%, then you can comfortably invest 2*5=10% of your principal in stocks and still be financially secure to pay for your expenses (assuming a loss of 20% of the 10% or a 2% loss). The Stock/Bond allocation is a common decision point. Robo advisors such as Betterment and WealthFront take your money and invest it in Stocks (Index or ETFs) vs. Bonds (Index or ETFs) based on your % allocation decision and then take a little off the top for doing that for you. The term 'robo' is used to denote that your payment and investment into preselected ETFs is 'automated' or you pay them and they invest for you. More sophisticated algorithms that decide which 'stock' to invest in are only found in quantitative hedge funds. The traditional online robo advisors decide which stock/bond allocation to use based on your age and risk tolerance. Slightly different concept regarding what 'robo' entails. There are similar balancing retirement funds as part of your 401K and are called something similar to 'Retirement Fund 2030' and another 'Retirement Fund 2040'. These are funds that slowly change the Stock/Bond allocation as you age so that by 2029 for one fund or 2039 for the other, the majority of investments are in Bonds.

We'll talk about Stocks and Bonds next. Mutual Funds and Hedge Funds will follow after that, just to give you a complete picture of the investing landscape. One important note to end this section is to discourage even thinking about 'full' broker-age firms. Discount ones like Fidelity and Charles Schwab among others allow you to trade stocks, ETFs, and other financial instruments for a 'dis-counted' price. On the other hand, full brokerage firms charge you fees that are a percentage% of your total investment account for opening an account, closing an account, talking to their advisors (emails are also charged), and a hefty percentage charge if a financial advisor with the brokerage firm is the one who clicks the button to buy or sell a stock that you tell them to buy or sell. One of my close friends worked with a full brokerage firm, and he asked my advice on what ETFs to buy. I told him what I had my money in, and he asked his advisor to set the same asset allocation. A year went by and we sold our positions in these particular ETFs. My friend then told me that he had been using a 'full' broker-age service and was charged 1.5% for buying an ETF and 1.5% for selling it. Poor guy barely made any returns above inflation for those two years and paid an additional 0.5% of his account each year just to have it 'maintained' or to keep it open. Investing in the same way that a full service brokerage or a robo advisor does requires only an extra few hours out of your entire year and you get to save a lot of fees in the process. It just requires a small commitment to your financial education.

STOCKS

A private company raises funds through debt by taking out loans or through equity by selling ownership shares of the company to private investors whether private equity investors, venture capitalists, or angel investors. When the company grows large enough that it wants a much larger amount of funds or to turn the founder's equity into tradable shares they go through an initial public offering (IPO) with any one of a number of exchanges that allow trading of company shares. The biggest ones are the NASDAQ and the NYSE (New York Stock Exchange). For the younger readers, the American Stock Exchange (AMEX) was the third largest exchange until it was acquired by the NYSE parent company. Once a company has undergone an IPO it is a publicly traded company. Buying shares on these large exchanges is possible through discount brokerage firms who pay these exchanges an access fee. Buying shares of any one company gives the buyer the opportunity to profit in the form of a stock price increase if the company's financials improve enough to attract more buyers to buy the company shares thereby increasing demand for a fixed supply and increasing the price of the stock. Holders of these common stocks have a claim to the company's assets in case it declares bankruptcy and is liquidated. This claim is secondary to fulfilling debt obligations to creditors and to shareholders who own preferred shares. Preferred shares are typically owned by the first private investors and sometimes can also be bought publicly. They are called preferred because they have preferences tied to them. Preferences can include a 2X preference where the investors get paid twice the money the invested in the event of a liquidation before any common shareholders receive any funds. If you are a common shareholder, you are unlikely to gain anything in the event of liquidation. Additionally, if you buy shares of a partnership which is common for oil drilling companies, you stand to lose money if the company goes bankrupt. The 2016 drop in oil prices because of a larger than expected supply and lower demand for oil caused many partnerships to declare chapter 11 bankruptcy. Chapter 7 bankruptcy is when the company close up shop and creditors never get their money, while Chapter 13 bankruptcy allows the debtor to keep their assets in exchange for paying part of their debts over the next 3 to 5 years. Chapter 11 is when they settle their debt and restructure into a new reorganized entity. Many oil Companies had enormous losses in

2016, and then in 2017 restructured and had their debt forgiven. However, because it is a partnership, any gains or losses are

Buying shares of stock that pay out quarterly dividends or also referred to as an annual yield pay out a percentage (typically 1-4%) of the stock price back to investors in the form of stock which means they reinvest the dividend back into the company. The premise behind dividends is to attract investors interested in fixed income for large companies that are unlikely to grow any larger. Smaller companies need the profit they make to re-invest in the company and so cannot give it away a portion of it as dividend back to the shareholders.

While individual stocks can be a great opportunity to build tremendous wealth, they are also extremely risky. Peter Thiel invested $500,000 in Facebook as a private angel investor in 2004 and in 2012 after the Facebook IPO his shares were worth a little over $1 billion. That's a 2000x return or an annual return of about 25,000%. Individual stocks can be very risky unless you know the industry, you understand financials, and have enough faith that the management of the company knows what it is doing. I will assume professional investing is not your day job, and that's why I don't recommend investing in individual stocks. If you like to gamble, you can always set aside 5% of your portfolio to invest in the next Facebook or Amazon. When

Amazon first had its IPO in 1997 its share price was $18 and in 2018 it went above $2000 a share or a 112X return. Still, that's the headliner that costly stock tips subscription services sell you. There are about 4000 stocks traded on NASDAQ and the NYSE and another 15,000 traded over the counter or OTC (which means they didn't need to meet the more stringent requirements of financial health needed to list on the larger exchanges). Statistically, we are unlikely to pick winners on every bet or even the majority of our bets. Still, if you'll get a thrill out of investing in these rockets, then limit it to a tiny portion of your retirement fund, the smaller portion the better.

INDEX FUNDS

An index fund is a mutual fund or ETF that follows an index by passively investing in the same stocks in an index. They were popularized more recently in the 1970s by economists and financial professionals who believed in a theory known as the efficient market hypothesis that states that all information is available to all investors at the same time and that is reflected in the price of the stock. In other words, there is no **inefficiency** in the market where one investor has a competitive advantage because they have information that someone else does not possess. Therefore, investors are unlikely to gain above-average returns and could return <u>below</u> average returns. With this belief, why not at least match the return of the market which is higher than inflation and therefore protects against inflation and increases the principle. The stock market as a whole returns 7% per year, the S&P 500 returns 8-10% per year, and the Nasdaq 100 returns 13% per year. Keep in mind that these

44

figures are based on decades of returns (with Nasdaq returns beginning only in 1985 because that is when the index was created). If we were to purposely pick a period between two recessions such as between 2001-2010 we would find returns between 1-3%! Keep that in mind. Index funds are a long term investment if you ride the waves, but can be a short term investment if you rebalance and move money from stocks to bonds before or during each market recession. One tell-tale sign is a rapid increase in returns right before a correction or recession in the index.

Index funds have expense ratios of 0.1-0.5% compared to more 'actively managed' mutual funds that charge expense ratios of 1-2% and have additional fees. Only a handful of mutual funds, about 15-20% outperform the market, but as we'll soon learn this is short lived, and moving your money from one winning mutual fund to another winning one significantly increases your odds of picking a loser over the long run. Over the long-term index funds outperform the majority (80% or more) of all actively managed funds.

In a classic investment book called 'A Random Walk Down Wall Street' by Burton Malkiel, he showed that a $10,000 investment in an index fund that follows the S&P 500 between 1969-1999 had a return of 31X compared to 17X for the average actively managed mutual fund.

We will learn more about ETFs and Mutual Funds but before we do that, let's pause to get more familiar with the different indexes--Note that the plural of index is indices but American financial publications unlike the rest of the world have popularized 'indexes' instead, so we'll use both in case you ever have a conversation with someone outside of the US.

The first stock average index was created on July 3rd, 1884 by Dow Jones & Company. The Dow Jones Industrial Average (DJIA) or the 'Dow' was created in 1896. The Dow is a price-weighted stock market index made up of 30 companies in the NYSE and NASDAQ. The reasoning behind creating the index according to Charles Dow was to get a measure of the economy as a whole. His company created hundreds of indices ever since but the first two were related to industrials and transportation (mainly railroad transportation at the time). Charles Dow believed that if both indices were moving up then the economy as a whole was moving up, and if one was moving up but the other moving down then that was a signal for change because industrials depend on transportation and vice versa. Of course that's not true today and the companies that make up the DJIA have changed over time. In fact 16% of the companies in the DJIA are technology companies compared to 50% or more in the Nasdaq 100 index.

Some of the top companies in the DJIA are:

1. Alcoa (NYSE: AA), an international producer of aluminium. Also included in the S&P 500.

2. DuPont (NYSE: DD), originally a gun powder producer during the American Civil War, today it is one of the largest chemical manufacturers whose brands include Teflon, Mylar, Kevlar, and others. DuPont has is the often referenced in classes on corporate governance and shady business practices as it has been the subject of multiple lawsuits for dumping chemicals in nearby waterways used to irrigate land and for drinking in small American communities. DD is also in the S&P 500 index.

3. ExxonMobil (NYSE: XOM), created by the merger of Exxon (Standard Oil of New Jersey) and Mobil (Standard Oil of New Jersey), both of which were 2 of the 34 companies that made up Standard Oil before it was ordered by the Supreme court in 1911 to split up into smaller companies because it was an illegal monopoly. The sheer size of Standard Oil is mind boggling. Chevron, BP, and Marathon were other daughter companies that emerged after the breakup. Standard had so much demand it had to export

kerosene to China in 1890 to supply lamp fuel to a population of 400 million. In fact, when Standard Oil broke up, the individual companies collectively were worth twice as much as the whole of the original company, making **John Davison Rockefeller's** net worth in 1913 equivalent to $410 billion in today's (2018) inflation adjusted dollars.

4. General Electric (NYSE: GE), was the result of a merger in 1892 between the Edison General Electric Company and the Thomson-Houston Electric Company. GE has expanded its business verticals significantly moving into higher growth industries such as aviation and healthcare, and as we know entertainment where it owns NBC universal. It had its ups and downs and was removed from the DJIA in 1924 for a year, then again in 1935, and again in 2018 when GE was kicked out and replaced with Walgreens.

The Standard & Poor's 500 or the S&P 500 is the most commonly used benchmark for the stock market as a whole. The S&P 500 is made of the 500 largest public companies and represents 70% of the total of the U.S. stock market. Originally developed in 1923 by Henry Varnum Poor of Poor's Publishing (I know not a great brand name for financial news). Poor's publishing merged with Standard Statistics in 1941 and in 1957 the S&P grew to 500 companies. Because it is based on the market capitalization of a company it is sector agnostic and therefore covers everything from technology, healthcare, financials, among other industries.

The Wilshire 5000 is also known as the total market index because it includes about 7000 securities, far greater than the S&P 500. It doesn't include thinly traded stocks (low volume, pink sheets) because their pricing data are not as accurate. However, because it does include small and medium cap stocks, during bull markets when the smaller cap stocks rise significantly, we can see the Wilshire 5000 have slightly higher returns than the S&P 500. For our purposes, it doesn't make much difference because even the mutual funds and ETFs that track the index only account for the top half of larger securities. The Wilshire 5000 was established by the Wilshire Associates in 1974. After an initial partnership with Dow Jones in 2004 that ended in 2009, the Wilshire 5000 is still calculated today by the Wilshire Associates. Similar to the S&P it reached an all-time high in 2000 then fell and didn't reach it again until 2007 then fell again and finally reached the same high of 2000 in 2013. Since then the index has almost doubled in value by 2018 which is remarkable but also worrisome for a correction.

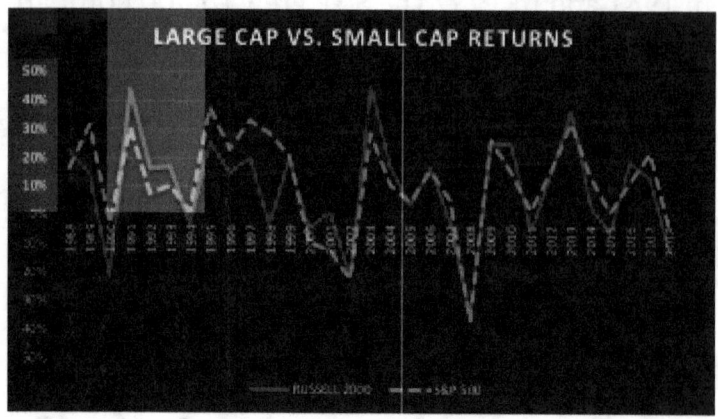

Russell 2000 is an index based on market capital-ization of the 2,000 smallest stocks in the Russell 3000 which tracks the 3,000 largest stocks by mar-ket capitalization (price times number of shares). In essence, it is an index of the bottom ⅔ of the largest 3000 companies. The Russell 2000 is a good indica-tor of the economic growth of small cap companies relative to large cap companies in the S&P 500. The graph above shows how closely the returns of the Russell 2000 follow the S&P 500 at an average cor-relation of 80%, and it also shows that the riskier small cap companies have higher peaks and lower troughs.

Nasdaq Composite Index is a market-capitalization weighted index of all the stocks trading on the NASDAQ stock exchange. Because the NASDAQ is popular with technology firms, more than half of the composite is made up of technology firms. Similar to the S&P 500, it peaked in 2000 and fell after the dot com bubble only to recover its 2000 level again in 2015 (slightly delayed to other indices). The Nasdaq 100 is a popular index tracking the top 100 companies which account for 90% of the value of the Nasdaq Composite. The popular FANG stocks are on NASDAQ and consist of Facebook (Nasdaq: FB), Amazon (Nasdaq: AMZN), Netflix (Nasdaq: NFLX) , and Google (Nasdaq: GOOGL). Where the FANG group goes, the rest of NASDAQ follows is the general theme, and that is why there are hundreds of ETFs and mutual funds that track the FANG group.

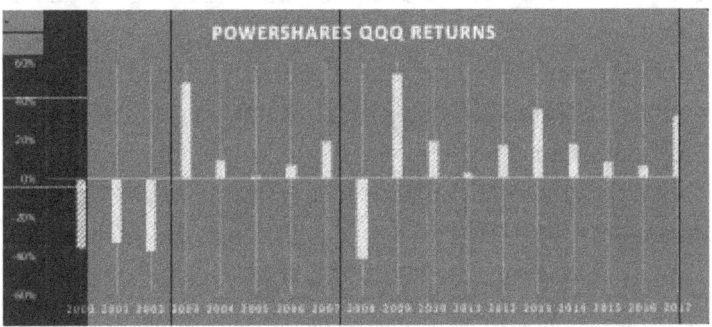

The Powershares QQQ ETF is one of the most popular ETFs and it tracks the Nasdaq 100 with a current market cap of $62 billion (2018).

Recently the Invesco cCompany is eliminating the Powershares brand, so you will find it listed as Invesco QQQ. Invesco is the 4th largest issuer of ETFs (measured by total assets under management), while the top three consist of BlackRock's iShares, Vanguard, and State Street Global Advisors.

This particular ETF lost 42% of its value in 2008 during the financial crisis but has since had positive returns every year for the next 9 years (average annual return of 20%). If you were to buy The QQQ ETF since its inception in 1999 (right before the dot com crash), you would still have had average annual returns of 6%. When it comes to this popular ETF, it seems that it has repetitive buying patterns. It appears that the single month of February in the six of the preceding eight bull years (2009-2017) with an average return of 4.65%. Similar patterns appear for July and again in October during the bull years. December and January appear to be the worst two months for QQQ. There could be a hundred different reasons that could explain this pattern of increased buying after the new year, in the summer, and before the holidays. Suffice to say, if you were thinking of buying QQQ, do so during the bull years, and potentially in the last week of January.

There are many foreign indices one could look at as well to get a feel for the international markets. England has the FTSE 100 (pronounced 'footsie') which is the Financial Times Share Index made up of the 100 largest companies in the London Stock Exchange (LSE) and weighted by market capitalization so larger companies carry more percentage weight in the index relative to smaller companies. Japan has the Nikkei 225 which tracks the largest 225 companies listed in the Tokyo Stock Exchange

(TSE) and is price-weighted. It used to be called the Nikkei Dow Jones Stock Average. If you're wondering how big these stock exchanges are relative to the US, it's interesting to note that the NYSE has a market cap of $23 trillion and the NASDAQ $11 trillion, compared to about $4 trillion each for the LSE and TSE. Also important to note as American Investors are increasingly beginning to follow international markets, the Euronext is the stock exchange of the European Union and has trading markets in Amsterdam, Brussels, London, Lisbon, Dublin, and Paris.

ETFS

Exchange Traded Funds or ETFs are a basket of shares in different companies in any asset class that can be traded in the public exchanges just like any individual stock. There are ETFs that mirror an index fund. The difference is that an index fund needs to be bought directly from the company that created it while an ETF is bought through your brokerage account. The S&P 500 was developed by S&P Dow Jones Indices which owns hundreds of indices. The S&P 500 index is based on the 500 largest companies by market capitalization or total number of shares multiplied by the share price. ETFs and mutual funds can follow an index very closely, and about 20% of funds do so.

John Bogle, an Economics graduate of Princeton University founded Vanguard Group in 1974 and created the first index investment trust in 1975 which was later renamed the Vanguard 500 Index Fund and tracked the S&P 500 index. In 2017 the

Vanguard 500 (VOO) returned 22% with an annual return of 8.4% in the prior 10 years and an expense ratio of 0.04%. Today, Edward Johnson III, son of Edward Johnson II who founded Fidelity Investments in 1949 was quoted at the time saying that he couldn't believe that "the great mass of investors are going to be satisfied with receiving just average returns". Well, today (2019) the Vanguard 500 holds about $400 Billion of investor's money.

Think of any type of industry and you'll find an ETF with shares from a basket of companies that represent it. If you want to invest in biotech companies in China, cannabis companies in Canada, or even an ETF that has a basket of international corporate bonds, you'll find it. Your sophistication with the different types of ETFs will grow with a small commitment to always be learning. In general, ETFs like mutual funds charge an expense ratio which is a percentage of the total value of your investment. Low expense ratios are about 0.1% and higher ones are closer to 0.5%. The average expense ratio of mutual has been falling largely because of pressure brought by low-cost ETFs. In fact, some analysts attribute the large gain the markets since the 2008 financial crisis largely due to the increasing popularity of ETFs.

Many discount brokerage firms have begun offering their own ETFs to members that are commission-free. Meaning you won't pay money to buy and sell them. You still pay the expense ratio which is slightly higher but you don't pay the $4-$8 per trade. These commission-free ETFs are a fantastic way to get involved in the stock market for the majority of investors. The minority of investors with several hundred thousand dollars to invest per trade may be better off choosing an ETF with a lower expense ratio that is not commission free. Leveraged ETFs which we'll discuss in a later section carry a higher expense ratio closer to 1% but they also have the potential for larger gains and losses.

The explosion of discount brokers in the past 30 years has created millions of amateur investors. Most of these offer the ability to open taxable accounts, individual retirement accounts (IRAs) and most are also capable of administering 401(k) plans for employers. In addition to providing the gamut of securities to trade, they also offer additional services such as robo investing, their own mutual funds, and their own ETFs. Examples of discount brokers include E-Trade, Charles Schwab, Fidelity, Ally Invest, Vanguard, and TD Ameritrade. One broker that is often missing from popular broker lists is Interactive Brokers. IB only has $86 billion in assets under management compared to Fidelity's $2.5 trillion, but it is the largest broker in terms of number of trades executed. The reason behind that is that IB was a pioneer and continues to be in the space of automated trading allowing day and swing traders to program automated trading strategies that continuously trade without their active management.

When deciding which ETFs to include in your portfolio, it's important to diversify into multiple asset classes especially if they are negatively correlated with each other so as to minimize your risk and exposure to any one asset class. For example, real estate, and commodities are weakly correlated with stocks while bonds tend to be negatively correlated with stocks. During a bear market, those weak positive and negative correlations can become moderate to strong positive correlations meaning that everything is dropping in price.

Let's look at a typical 60/40 portfolio made up of 60% stocks and 40% bonds. In the 1990s, the average return was 14% while volatility was 9%. After the financial crisis, returns of a 60/40 portfolio dropped to 7% with similar volatility of 9%. In other words, the stock/bond correlations changed, and they often change. When you're younger (20s and 30s) you can afford to an 80/20 stock/bond split. As you near retirement, that should change over-time to 20/80 stock/bond split. Of course, you can rebalance at any time and it is prudent to do so every few years.

There are many ETFs to help diversify your investments. I suggest that you use your background when it comes to investing. For example, if your family business is jewellery and you have experience buying and selling gold, then consider studying multiple gold and silver commodity ETFs.

Let's look at several different types of ETFs to give you a sense of what is available.

Index ETFs:
- SPDR S&P 500 (SPY) tracks the S&P 500 index with a low expense ratio of 0.09%.
- Vanguard S&P 500 (VOO) tracks the S&P 500 index and has a low expense ratio of 0.04%.
- SPDR Dow Jones Average (DIA) tracks the DJIA index
- Vanguard Total Stock Market ETF (VTI) also tracks the DJIA index.
- iShares Russell 2000 (IWM) tracks the Russell 2000 index
- Invesco QQQ (QQQ) track the Nasdaq 100
- iShares Core US Aggregate Bond (AGG) is the largest bond ETF in the world and tracks the Barclays Aggregate U.S. Bond Index which itself includes corporate bonds, municipal bonds, and US treasury (i.e government) bonds. Expense ratio is only 0.05%.
- iShares MSCI EAFE (EFA) tracks the MSCI EAFE index which includes 900 international stocks in developed market equities, excluding the U.S. and Canada. The EAFE stands for Europe, Australasia, and Far East.
- Vanguard FTSE Emerging Markets ETF

(VWO) tracks the FTSE Emerging Markets All Cap China A Inclusion Index. This index tracks stocks from more than 20 emerging-market countries.

Sector ETFs:

- VanEck Vectors Oil Services (OIH) tracks the MVIS® U.S. Listed Oil Services 25 Index (MVOIHTR).
- SPDR Financial Select Sector Fund (XLF) tracks the Financial Select Sector Index which consists of the financial companies within the S&P 500. Note that XLF tends to be a leading indicator meaning that if the XLF moves from an uptrend to a downtrend while the S&P 500 is still in an uptrend, then that is a sign that the S&P 500 could soon follow in the downtrend. This is known as bearish divergence, something we talk about in technical trading. TLT is another financial ETF that is very popular.
- Vanguard Real Estate (VNQ) tracks the MSCI US Investable Market Real Estate 25/50 Index. Schwab US REIT ETF (SCHH) which tracks the Dow Jones U.S. Select REIT Index.
- Fidelity MSCI Energy ETF (FENY) tracks the MSCI USA IMI Energy Index
- Invesco S&P 500 Equal Weighted Health Care ETF (RYH) tracks the healthcare companies within the S&P 500.

Commodities ETFs

- SPDR Gold Shares (GLD) & iShares Gold

Trust (IAU) buy and store gold thus closely tracking gold prices. 2017 was a phenomenal year for gold ETFs with returns of 11-12%.

- Aberdeen Standard Physical Silver Shares ETF (SIVR) buys silver bullion and thus closely track price of silver.
- Teucrium Wheat ETF (WEAT) buys wheat futures contracts traded on the Chicago Board of Trade.
- United States Oil (USO) invests in futures contracts for crude oil, diesel-heating oil, gasoline, natural gas, and other petroleum-based fuels.
- United State Natural Gas (UNG) invests in futures contracts for natural gas that are traded on the NYMEX, and ICE Futures.
- iShares Core MSCI EAFE (IEFA)
- **iShares MSCI EAFE (EFA), AUM $77 Billion:** EFA is the biggest ETF that invests in international stocks. The fund tracks the MSCI EAFE index, which includes over 900 stocks outside of the United States. The expense ratio for EFA is 0.32 percent.
- **Vanguard FTSE Developed Markets ETF (VEA), AUM $71 Billion:** VEA tracks the FTSE Developed All Cap ex-US Index, which represents approximately 3,700 common stocks of large-, mid-, and small-cap companies located in Canada and the major markets of Europe and the Pacific region. Other countries include Japan, United Kingdom, Germany, Switzerland, and Australia. Expenses for VEA are 0.07 percent.
- **Vanguard FTSE Emerging Markets ETF**

(VWO), AUM $68 Billion: VWO tracks the FTSE Emerging Markets All Cap China A Inclusion Index, which represents large-, mid-, and small-cap stocks of companies located in emerging markets around the world. Expenses for VWO are 0.14 percent.

- **iShares Core MSCI EAFE (IEFA), AUM $56 Billion:** IEFA is another ETF to make our list that tracks the MSCI EAFE, which includes stock of companies in non-U.S. countries in Europe, Japan and Australia. Expenses for IEFA are 0.08 percent.

MUTUAL FUNDS

U nlike ETFs, mutual funds are 'actively managed' by a fund manager and a team of financial analysts. The goal of mutual funds is to return above average returns, and they quantify that by benchmarking against an index such as the S&P 500 index.

The fund manager along with his or her team conducts financial analysis and decides to invest the fund's portfolio into stocks, bonds, or other investment vehicles. The stocks that the fund owns and the percentage weight of each stock relative to the rest of the portfolio is detailed in the **fund prospectus**-- available to review before investing in any particular mutual fund.

Mutual funds can also passively track stock or bond market indices by buying the same or a majority of the same stocks in any particular index. Since the average investor cannot directly invest in an index fund, when we talk about investing in 'index' funds we are talking about investing in mutual funds or ETFs that track an index such as the S&P 500.

Unlike an ETF, a mutual fund can't be bought and sold any time of day. Instead, the mutual fund calculates the Net Asset Value or NAV at the end of the trading day which sets the price of a share of that mutual fund, and any buy or sell orders are executed after the market close.

Non-index mutual funds are actively managed and therefore require higher fees. More recently, some ETFs have a tiny bit of active management in the sense that they remove stocks that are low quality or high volatility based on a predetermined set of criteria. These 'actively managed' ETFs charge a slightly higher management fee (0.5% for example). I put 'actively managed' in quotations because it's mostly algorithmic and automated.

To purchase a mutual fund through your brokerage account, whether through a taxable account that you own or a tax deferred account such as an IRA or Roth IRA, you will face two types of fees. The first is the **expense ratio** which we talked about and for actively managed funds can range from 1-2% of your investment per year on average. The expense ratio is not paid upfront but rather is deduced from the fund's returns to pay the fund manager's salary, expenses for marketing the fund to potential investors (12b-1 fees), and other service charges such as the transaction cost of buying and selling stocks on an active basis. Then there are fees when you buy into and sell out of a mutual fund known as the **load** fees. This is similar to some of the products of a full brokerage accounts and is intended to keep the money with the mutual fund. A **front load** fee is a percentage of your investment charged just to buy into the fund. A **back-end load** fee or a sales charge is another fee that represents a percentage of your investment. Some back-end load fees are structured so that if you sell your mutual fund shares after the 5th or 10th year then there is back-end fee but if you sell earlier, then you incur this penalty. Both the front and back-end load fees can range between 3-6%. Some of the newer (less popular) mutual funds and index mutual funds are 'no-load' funds or in other words only charge an expense ratio fee. If I had the opportunity to invest with a legendary fund manager, and assuming I meet the minimum to invest in their fund, then I would be comfortable with the load fees, but for the majority of funds available, I would not even consider a fund with load fees.

We know that about 80% of actively managed funds underperform the market. Picking the 20% that will in the future outperform the market is a guessing game and the odds are 1 to 5. Additionally, several studies have shown that after 5 years of active management only ⅕ of funds that beat or outperformed the market continue to do so for the next 5 years. This pattern continues so that after 10 years of successfully outperforming the market only $\frac{1}{5}$ of those funds continue to do so over the subsequent 5 years. That means your odds of picking the fund manager that will outperform the market for 15 years is $\frac{1}{5}*\frac{1}{5}*\frac{1}{5}*= 1$ to 125 or a 0.8% chance of picking the winner.

BONDS

B onds are debt instruments also known as a form of debt financing. A company can raise funds to finance its growth through equity financing or debt financing. Equity financing is through the sale of stock and debt financing is through the selling of corporate bonds. These IOUs carry with them ratings based on the health of the business and the likelihood of the business declaring bankruptcy and defaulting on repaying these loans. The riskier corporate bonds are known as Junk bonds and have a higher interest rate return as expected.

Companies are not the only entities that need debt financing. Local government raise funds through municipal funds. The government itself sells bonds backed by the US treasury, hence why they are called US Treasury bonds. Each entity can set a specific interest rate. US treasury bonds have the lowest interest rates but are the safest. Government bonds have a lower yield and are less likely to default unless the government defaults, but it hasn't yet with a national debt of $22 trillion and climbing. This is because the government has the magical ability to print money! If it couldn't, it would default today because no nation or group of nations is able to loan the US $22 trillion.

A bond might sell for $1000 which is another way of saying it has a par or **face value** of $1000. Each bond can decide to pay interest also known as the **coupon rate** once a year (annually) or twice a year (semi-annually). In addition to interest paid to the bond-holder, the price of the bond itself can change over time depending on the government (well the Federal Reserve) setting new interest rates. The longer the **term** of the bond, the higher the **yield** (or annual interest return), but also the higher the risk that interest rates might go up. A longer time horizon means more opportunity for the Federal Reserve to come up with a reason to raise interest rates. If interest rates go up, the price of the bond decreases and therefore the yield which is a percentage return on the price of the bond is smaller--in absolute terms. This inverse relationship is factored into Duration which is the remaining term length of the bond and is a measure of the sensitivity of a bond to the interest rate. A bond with a duration of 3 years means that its price would fall by 3% when interest rates go up by 1%. For example if a $1000 bond with coupon rate of 5% paid annually (so yield = coupon rate) has a duration of 3 years and we find out that interest rate went up 1% and other bonds are now being sold with coupon rates of 6%. For our bond to become attractive again, it has to sell at a discount. Since its duration is 3 years, then the face value should decrease so that a $970 discount bond with coupon rate of 5% is similarly attractive to a $1000 bond with a coupon rate of 6%.

We can buy treasury bonds, notes, and bills directly from the US treasury at **https://treasurydirect.gov** . Or we can buy an ETF that buys them. What's the difference between, bills, notes, and bonds? The time to maturity is the difference. **Treasury bills** have a duration of one year or less. You could buy a 26 week treasury bill for example. These bills are similar to a zero-coupon bond because they a coupon rate of 0%. Effectively, treasury bills are sold at a discount of their face value and you receive the face value upon maturity. So for example, a $100 US treasury 26 week bill might sell for $98.5. After 26 weeks, you'll get $100 which means you made 100/98.5=1.5%! **Treasury notes** have durations of 2 to 10 years while **Treasury bonds** have durations longer than 10 years. The 30 year Treasury bond has the highest yield because it has such a long duration. It usually pays around 3% annually or 1.5% semi-annually. The problem of course with 30 year terms is that it doesn't protect you against inflation. If inflation went up higher than the 3% yield you're stuck with each year, then the purchasing power of your investment just decreased. **Inflation risk** is a serious problem with longer term bonds.

When evaluating bonds to include in your portfolio, the easiest method is to use one of a hundred different bond ETFs. Alternatively, you could invest in municipal bonds in your state or city which have the added benefit of waiving local taxes on gains. Note that state taxes are waived for treasury bonds. Unfortunately, interest received from corporate bonds is taxed at the local, state, and federal level.

Lastly, and very importantly, if you want to hedge again a rise in inflation you should consider investing in TIPS or Treasury Inflation-Protected Securities. TIPS are bonds that have a variable return which consists of a fixed return (1-2% for example) in addition to the current rate of inflation. Many funds have a large weighting towards TIPS and therefore you do not need to invest in TIPS directly, but can do so by proxy through a TIPS-heavy ETF. Vanguard offers the Vanguard Inflation-Protected Securities Fund Investor Shares or VIPSX with an expense ratio of 0.2% and average annual returns of 4-5%. VIPSX invests in more than 43 bonds with an average effective maturity of 8.2 years and duration of 7.5 years with average yield to maturity of 3%.

ALTERNATIVE INVESTMENTS

While investing in real estate is considered an alternative investment, we have discussed the potential of participating in ETFs or mutual funds that invest in REITs or Real Estate Investment Trusts as a proxy for investing directly into real estate. REITs can be private or publicly traded on a stock exchange. Publicly traded REITs pool investor funds and buy properties to manage or rehab and sell. The reason investing in funds that track the real estate markets is an option for increasing diversification as another asset class in addition to stocks and bonds is because historically real estate has not been correlated with the stock or bond market (except in the 2008 housing crisis).

The Vanguard Real Estate ETF (VNQ) invests in REITs with a low expense ratio of 0.12% and annual return of 7.77% since inception in 2004. Its expense ratio is low because it follows an real estate index. In 2017, it made the switch from the MSCI US REIT Index to the MSCI US Investable Market Real Estate 25/50 which includes real estate management, development companies, and REITs thereby broadening the exposure to the real estate market.

Additionally, Hedge funds, private equity funds, and venture capital funds all fall under the category of truly alternative investments. The problem is that they rarely beat the market, they turn the fund managers into some of the richest people in America, and require you to be an <u>accredited</u> investor in order to qualify as a limited partner or investor in these funds. Hedge funds were attractive for the wealthy because of something known as the Sharpe ratio. The Sharpe ratio gives us the risk-adjusted return of a portfolio of stocks. For example, let's say our 60/40 stock/bond portfolio returns 14%. We subtract that from what we could have achieved without any risk such as investing in the US treasury bonds. We get 14-3 = 11% return above this risk-free rate. Now, we divide this by the standard deviation of returns from all the stocks in the portfolio which is a measure of volatility. Let's say volatility for a 60/40 stock/bond portfolio is 9%, therefore our Sharpe ratio is 11/9 = 122%. Let's say that if the hedge fund handled our 60/40 stock/bond portfolio their return after they take their cut would be 12% instead of the 14% I would have received if I invested directly in the stock market. Well, hedge funds would not have been popular if they weren't able to lower risk. This particular hedge fund handling my money has a volatility of 6% instead of 9%. The new Sharpe ratio is therefore (12-3) % / 6% = 150% which is higher than the previous ratio of 122%. On a risk adjusted basis, the hedge fund is safer. In a bull market it will have a lower return, and in a bear market it will have a smaller loss. Investing in hedge funds is not something the average investor will be thinking about, but for the future wealthy readers, this is just one form of an alternative investment.

RECOMMENDED LEARNING TOOL

https://tools.finra.org/fund_analyzer/

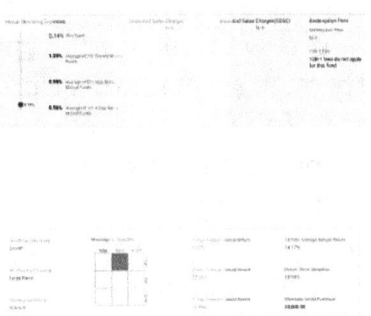

Vanguard 500 Index Fund Investor Shares (VFINX)

F INRA, the Financial Industry Regulatory Authority is a private self-regulatory organization (SRO) that regulates brokerage firms and financial products sold in exchange markets. FINRA

Peter Oliver

administrates many of the licensing exams that brokers, financial analysts, and other finance professionals required to be allowed to work. FINRA regulations are enforced by the government SEC, the Securities and Exchange Commission, which is the ultimate regulator and prosecutor in the securities industry.

That being said, they have a free tool that allows you to search and compare more than 30,000 different funds--ETFs or Mutual funds across multiple different asset classes including domestic equities, international equities, and the bond market. Online brokerage firms have similar search and index tools but if you're just new to this world, it may be worthwhile to go through several different funds to start getting a sense of the differences in performances, fees, and the financial instruments they invest in. If you are just browsing, there are filters you could use for product type and Prospectus Objective. If you're just starting out, then you could pick only a handful of ETFs in different asset classes and with stop losses in places until you grow more comfortable taking decisions on your behalf. Alternatively, you could still meet with a financial advisor but now you should be better informed to have a fruitful conversation when it comes to your needs for retirement.

Another helpful tool is the US News catalog of most of the available ETFs. I would take the rankings with

74

a grain of salt, but it helps focus your attention to categorizing ETFs in terms of whether they follow bonds, large indices like the S&P, emerging market indices, specific sector indices, commodities, or even alternative investment ETFs. The most recent link to the rankings and categories can be found here: **https://money.usnews.com/funds/etfs/**

TECHNICAL
ANALYSIS

Technical Analysis the study of price movement and what it tells us about the behavior of the market. Momentum trading is one that trades based on the momentum which is the price and volume action of a stock that causes it to follow a trend--an uptrend, a downtrend, or a sideways trend. One of the oldest trend indicators is the simple moving average which plots the average price over a fixed number of periods thereby smoothing out the price chart and giving us a clear indication if the trend is up, down, or sideways. We'll learn much more regarding technical analysis in the next guide in the series, but in this book I want to make sure to at least share with you the common practice of comparing a short-term and a long-term moving average.

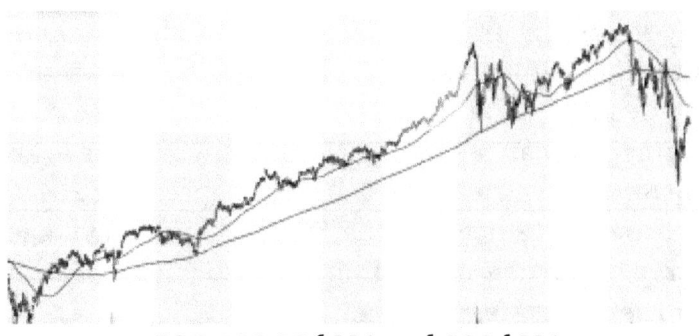

S&P 500 50d MA and 200d MA

Moving averages are very commonly compared to each other predict short term trend reversals. Some of the oldest technical traders are happy and achieve their desired returns by using only the 50 day and the 200 day moving average. If the shorter 50 day moving average crosses above the 200 day moving average then that is a bullish signal that after another several periods the 200 day moving average will follow the uptrend. If the shorter 50 day moving average crosses below the 200 day moving average, then that is a bearish signal that after several more periods the 200 day moving average will show the same downtrend. Why not just follow the 50 day moving average since it is shorter and more reactive? Well, if you want to get a feel for the longer term trends in the market, then it helps to see if the price action is overall bullish or overall bearish, and it is the relative action of the shorter and longer term moving averages that can give us this forecast. In the S&P 500 price chart above we see the 50 day moving average cross over the 200 day moving average in March, 2016 and stay above it until December, 2018. As long as the 50 day moving average remained above the 200 day moving average, we can see the S&P 500 price continue in an uptrend between March 2016 and September 2018. October 2018 is when the 50 day moving average curve began down trending and also when the S&P 500 began its steep decline.

BEAR MARKETS

F irst and foremost, I'd like to stress the importance of taking money out of the market when it appears the bull run has lost steam. When we talk about 'the market' we are usually referring to a major index like the DJIA or the S&P 500. A correction in the market is when one or more of these indices lose 10% of their value or experience a 10% price decrease. A bear market is one where there is a 20% price decrease. Are these arbitrary? Yes. The S&P 500 could lose 15% of its value and we analysts would say the market is in correction, but the S&P 500 follows the 500 largest companies and is weighted by market cap. It does not represent the entire market. In fact, often times when the S&P 500 is in correction territory and on its way to confirm a bear market, the Russell 2000 which follows 'small cap' companies has already lost 20% of its value.

The S&P 500 index had 22 corrections in total since

1945 and 12 bear markets. Some bear markets had 2 corrections in the same year such as the two corrections in 2018. Roughly, all told, there is a 40% chance corrections turn into bear markets.

The last bear market lasted 17 months and ran from October 2007 until March 2009 dropping the S&P 500 by 57%. On average, bear markets last 14 months but it can be much shorter (3 months in 1990) or much longer (61 months from 1937 until March, 1942). Bull markets on the other hand average 4.5 years between corrections.

Because these bear markets can last a long time, and can potentially wipe out gains that took years to become realized, being cognizant of your options during bear markets is important. Again, the best and safest method is to pull your money out of the market and re-enter the market on the next 4-8 year bull run. Alternatively, your other options are moving your money into another asset class that is inversely correlated with the stock market, moving your retirement funds into fixed income from government backed bonds, or betting against the market using put options, shorting the market, or buying inverse ETFs. You don't have to move your entire portfolio, you can always change your asset allocation from stocks to a higher proportion into safer bonds or another asset class. Unless you are a sophisticated investor, do not try and beat the stock market in a bear market.

PUT OPTIONS

Options are similar to the options contract we discussed in the Real Estate Series where you pay for the option to buy the asset by some deadline in the future. In the stock market, if your discount brokerage firm has activated options trading for your account, you are allowed to pay for the option to buy a specific stock at a specific strike price by a specific date known as the expiration date of the option. Paying for the option to buy a stock is known as a call option. Paying for the option to sell a stock at a specific price is known as a put option. If before the expiration date, the price of the stocks moves above the strike price of your call option, you have the right to exercise the option, buy the stock at the lower strike price, then sell it back in the market at the higher price. You don't have to buy the stock, in fact you could sell the call option back to the options market for someone else to exercise it. If you don't exercise the option, then the most you lost is the cost to buy the option. For call options, the longer the expiration date, and the closer the strike price is to the current price, the more expensive the option contract is. Each contract contains 100 shares, and the cost per share in the option contract can be anywhere from a few cents to a few dollars but always a fraction of the actual stock price. The same logic applies for put options. The longer the expiration date and the closer the strike price is to the current price, the more expensive the option contract becomes.

Option Chain for SPDR S&P 500 (SPY)

Calls	Last	Chg	Bid	Ask	Vol	Open Int	Root	Strike	Puts	Last	Chg	Bid	Ask	Vol	Open Int
Jun 19, 2020	38.55		37.12	37.55	0	116	SPY	235	Jun 19, 2020	13.11	0.11	12.98	13.15	490	1815
Jun 19, 2020	34.21	2.46	33.70	34.10	6	52	SPY	240	Jun 19, 2020	14.23	-0.45	14.38	14.58	94	974
Jun 19, 2020	31.94		30.38	30.76	0	491	SPY	245	Jun 19, 2020	15.92		15.92	16.12	0	300
Jun 19, 2020	28.78		27.19	27.56	0	374	SPY	250	Jun 19, 2020	17.53	-0.31	17.59	17.80	9	5483
Jun 19, 2020	25.68		24.17	24.50	0	1594	SPY	255	Jun 19, 2020	19.58		19.41	19.64	0	7915
Jun 19, 2020	21.73	-1.16	21.28	21.59	1	1329	SPY	260	Jun 19, 2020	21.26	-0.53	21.39	21.66	31	2371
Jun 19, 2020	18.85	-0.61	18.56	18.86	3	237	SPY	265	Jun 19, 2020	23.32	-0.20	23.56	23.64	1	329
Jun 19, 2020	16.43	-0.53	16.04	16.31	3	1137	SPY	270	Jun 19, 2020	26.02	0.30	25.92	26.23	3	229
Jun 19, 2020	14.70		13.71	13.98	0	678	SPY	275	Jun 19, 2020	30.53		28.49	28.83	0	1562
Jun 19, 2020	11.79	-0.53	11.59	11.81	5	719	SPY	280	Jun 19, 2020	30.27		31.29	31.67	0	148

Let's go through an example. Let's imagine we want to buy a put option on the S&P 500 assuming that the bear market will last until June 2020. Since the S&P 500 is an index, we need to use its proxy such as the SPY ETF which has options available for specific date. Fortunately, they have an option chain for June 2020. The highlighted box indicates 'in the money' options or the most expensive options because they are closest to the current price. On the left we have our call options and the right our put options. Each row shows a different strike price which is shown in the middle column. Let's decide (based on some technical analysis) that the price is likely to fall to $235 (though potentially as low as $155) before June 2020. We would then buy the June 2020 put option for a strike price of $240 where the last price was $14.23/share. Because a contract is 100 shares, we would pay $1423 which is known as the premium. If the price falls to $155 before June 2020 and we exercise our option, then our profit would be $240-$155= $85 per share, or $8500 per contract minus our $1423 premium for a net profit of $7077. Most people who trade options lose money. Trading options can be very complex with multiple combinations of puts and calls to reduce risk. Investors who offer their shares in the options market price them cleverly enough to maximize the opportunity to make money off the premium. If the price never goes above the strike price (in a call option) or below the strike price (in a put option) the options trader is forced to forfeit their right to exercise the option, and the premium is transferred to the bank account of the option writer. Beginner investors should not trade these without practicing with small amounts first and continuing to educate themselves on the risks involved. I mention it here to show you one of the many ways to bet against the market.

SHORT SELLING

If you haven't seen it yet, I highly recommend watching the movie 'The Big Short' which is based off of the Michael Lewis (another favorite author) of the same name. Christian Bale is brilliant, and unexpected but we also see Brad Pitt and Steve Carell starring in this very serious movie about the how one person saw the housing crisis taking shape long before the markets took notice. What does it mean to short a stock? It basically means you borrow the stock from your brokerage firm and sell it to the market at its current price. Now you owe the broker these shares of stock, so you must buy them back from the market at some point in the future. Investors who short stock assume the price will decline and they can then buy the stock from the market at a lower price, keep the difference (between selling it at a higher price and buying at a lower price), then return the shares borrowed back to the broker. Short selling is possible with a margin account which is available in taxable accounts but not in retirement accounts as most brokers prevent people from risking their retirement accounts. I don't short stocks, instead I prefer investing in inverse ETFs which we'll talk about next.

I describe short selling because I want to clarify a misconception that I've seen in blogs, forums, and even a book on momentum trading I picked up by a guy with 30 years of experience trading stocks. In all these mediums of communication, the discount short selling as too little reward for the risk. Let's understand risk first. If the stock you shorted continue to move in price, theoretically it can go to infinity on the upside (not realistically, but theoretically). That means that at some point and probably sooner than you want to, the broker will require you to buy back the shares of stock if the price is not moving the direction you want. If you shorted a stock at $100 and it went to $300, the broker requires you to buy the shares back or to fund your margin account with additional funds. If you buy the shares back at $300, you have a $200 loss per share. On the other hand, if you bought a stock outright for $100 and it went to zero, you only lost $100 or the value you invested. Therefore, short selling is riskier than buying a stock outright. Ok, the argument then goes that if the risk is so high, why short a $100 stock when the maximum return you can make is 100% if it goes to zero, whereas if you go long (invest for the long-term) on a stock, then it can appreciate by 100%, 200%, or 1000% in the case of some technology stocks. Let me pause here for a second and see if you picked up on the misconception.

If your reward is limited relative to your risk, then no smart hedge fund manager would waste time and money letting the world know (especially on financial news media) that they are shorting a stock. It must stand to reason that they expect a very large return. In fact, they make these large bets when they especially believe the stock will go to zero and there's interesting math behind it. A failed anecdote is that of Bill Ackman, manager of Pershing Square Capital Management who shorted Herbalife (HLF) at $45 dollars for a lump sum of $1 billion. Ackman believed Herbalife was a pyramid scheme and once he told enough people, everyone would sell their shares, and he would go down in history as one of the best investors of all time. Unfortunately, few sold their shares, and HLF went from $45 to $92 before Ackman finally bought the shares back and closed his short position. Another but this time more successful anecdote took place in September 17, 1992 also known as 'Black Wednesday'. The British Pound had joined a fixed exchange rate, but it was priced incorrectly relative to the Deutschmark. The people knew it and the British government said it would buy up the British Pound to keep it within its range until they sorted out their deficits and interest rates. They couldn't raise interest because of a recent recession. Well George Soros, the manager of the Quantum Fund (founded in 1970) was 62 years old at the time and he had read comments from German Central Bank Officials that the sterling's fixed price may need to be readjusted. He shorted the British pound to the tune of $10 billion dollars. In the morning of the September 17, 1992, the British Government bought $27 billion dollars' worth of their currency in hopes of eliminating the short pressure. That didn't work because other hedge funds saw what Soros did and joined his ranks in shorting the British pound. The British government announced it would raise interest rate by 5% from 10% to 15% but that had no effect on the number of units of the currency being sold. Eventually, the British government announced they would move from a fixed exchange to a floating exchange, and after the transition the price continued to drop. The Quantum Fund made about $7 billion from this one short, and Soros himself netted about $1.4 billion has his 'cut' of the profits.

So let's see why it's lucrative to short a stock when you have a lot of confidence that it is worth much less than its current price. If you short a stock at $100 and it goes to zero, you DO NOT make 100% return. If the stock price drops to $50 and you buy it then and pocket the difference from selling borrowed shares at $100 and buying shares at $50, you made $50 after buying the stock for $50 or 100% return. The lower the price drop, the return increase exponentially. Let's assume the price dropped by another half to $25, if you exit your short position, the profit would be $75 or 300% of your $25 purchase. What about if it was $12.5? Then exiting the position at that price point would return $87.5 per share or 700% return. What about if the price dropped all the way down to $1? That's a $99/share return or a 9,900% return! Do you now see why it is very much worth the time and money to let the world know what a big scam a company is which you also happen to be shorting? This is still very risky because you would need true asymmetric information, information that the rest of the market has not yet caught on to for this to be massively successful. For smaller gains, you can short an ETF that tracks the index during a bear market.

INVERSE ETFS

I nverse ETFs move up when their counterpart moves down and vice versa. Most major ETFs have inverse ETFs, and major sectors and indices also have inverse ETFs you can invest in. There are also some ETFs described as leveraged ETFs. This means that the ratio of price movement is not 1:1 but rather 2:1 or 3:1 relative to the index or ETF it is inverse to. These are riskier. Two of my favorite ETF/Inverse ETF pairs are QQQ which tracks the Nasdaq 100 index, and SQQQ which is a 3x leveraged inverse ETF. If QQQ goes down by 1%, SQQQ goes up by 3%. Warren Buffett always said invest in what you know. Otherwise you're gambling. When it comes to investing in inverse ETFs during a bear market, it's better to have been following that ETF for a number of months before hand. Every investor has a universe of stocks they follow daily or weekly so they can start to build a 6th sense in terms of what the normal patterns of buying and selling pressures look like as well as the normal volatility for a particular stock. I follow about 20 ETFs for my retirement account that continues to change every year as my sophistication grows. I'll share a few inverse ETFs that you could look up online or discuss with others as you begin to build your investor sophistication level. The ones I list here are riskier because of increased leverage. Note that there are multiple ETF providers (Direxion, Velocityshares, Proshares, etc) and they can refer to inverse ETFs as 'inverse', 'short', or 'bear' as opposed to 'bull', and 'long'

SPXS (NYSE): Direxion Daily S&P 500 Bear 3X Shares
SQQQ (Nasdaq): ProShares UltraPro Short QQQ. Note this is a 3X leverage.
DWT (NYSE): VelocityShares 3x Inverse Crude Oil ETN
ZBIO (Nasdaq): ProShares UltraPro Short NASDAQ Biotechnology
YANG (NYSE): Direxion Daily FTSE China Bear 3X Shares. This is the inverse of the large index FTSE China 50 Index. Amusingly, the alternative ETF is the YINN ETF or Direxion Daily FTSE China Bull 3X Shares.

FINAL REMARK

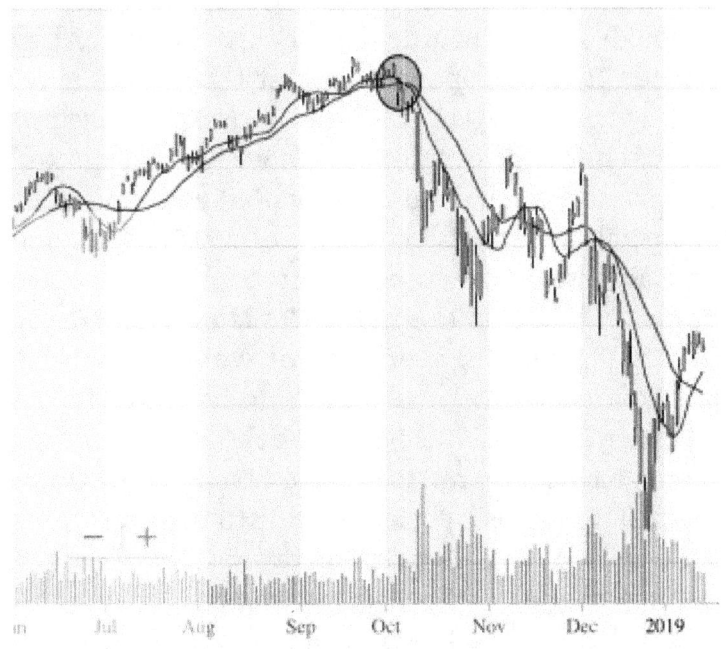

Short Moving Average Cross Over (and
under) Long Moving Average

Hopefully, you have a conservative financial advisor who can advise you when it is better to rebalance your asset allocation or liquidate your accounts or even secure retirement through a fixed income annuity that we described earlier. If you happen to look at the 50 day moving average and the 200 day moving average as shown in the prior figure when we discussed moving averages, you would have called your broker or financial advisor in December of 2018 after some initial losses. If you used a shorter moving average to spot trends in 'the market', such as the 10 day and 20 day moving averages, you would see a figure as shown above where you would have caught the 10 day moving average crossing the 20 day moving average to a lower price in the first week of October, 2018 which is perfect timing to liquidate your stocks. HOWEVER, with shorter moving averages, we see the 10 day MA crossover the 20 day MA multiple times in the past year alone. That's why longer period moving averages are used to show the general trend. As you gain more experience, you will start to build the vocabulary and recognize patterns in the market that make you pick up the phone and call your financial advisor and eventually one day to just manage your retirement account yourself. It is impossible to accurately to predict the future but building knowledge and a background in investments will allow you to avoid bigger losses and maximize your gains.

CONCLUSION

Have a plan and a strategy.

J ust like going on trip in your car, it is important that investors have a plan and a destination in mind before investing their money. Your goals —whether planning for retirement or buying a home—dictate your time horizon, which dictates your tolerance for risk. Additionally, you want to make sure that you diversify your investments so that some do well when the rest of your portfolio might not. This approach allows an investor to construct a portfolio that is in line with their risk tolerance and that balances potential return with some downside risk protection.

In terms of 2019 and 2020, no one knows for sure what will happen but my suspicion is that the market will continue to decline after a run up which is a good time to either keep your retirement fund (if you control it through an IRA) out of the market, increase the ratio of bonds in your portfolio, or invest in inverse ETFs that go up when the market goes down. In the next guide, which should only be read by readers with a higher risk tolerance, we'll learn that the stock price chart pattern shown below of the returns of the S&P 500 index is known as a head and shoulders pattern which is a signal for continued price declines. These charts are called 'relative' charts in that they are relative to the price. I modified the price chart by taking the percentage returns of each index for each year and plotting it against time.

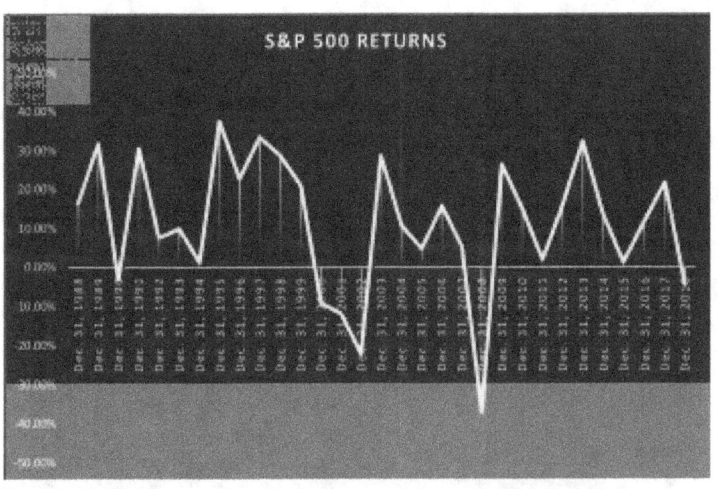

A similar pattern is seen in the other indices

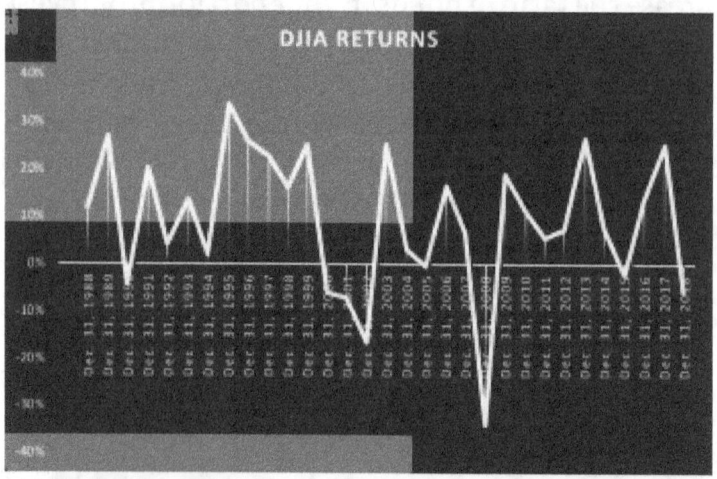

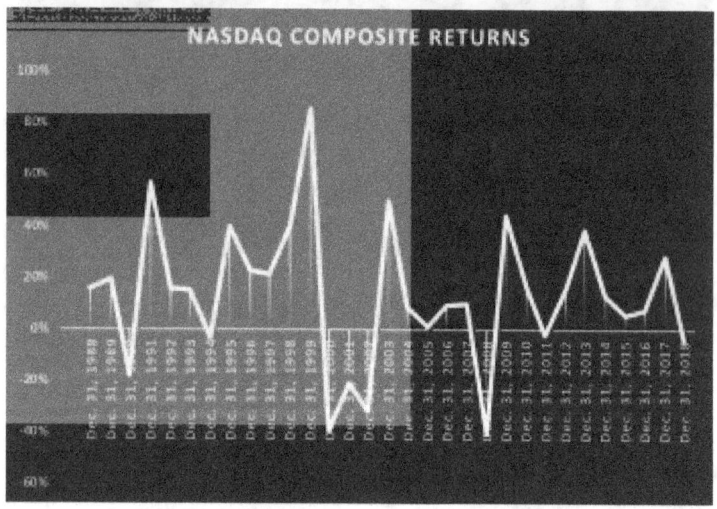

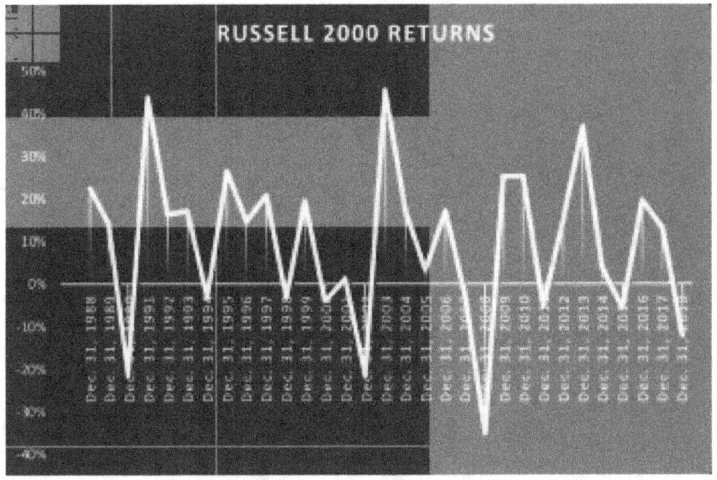

In late 2020 or 2021, again while no one knows for sure what will happen, usually after a bear market we have several years of a bull market with significant returns and that is an opportunity to put money back into the market or change your stock to bond ratio.

This is only the first step, and hopefully a concise one, in a life-long path of education. Always be learning.

--- The End ---

To join the discussion and interact with other Concise Reads readers, please join the free online community at **https://www.concisereads.com**

www.ingramcontent.com/pod-product-compliance
Lightning Source LLC
Chambersburg PA
CBHW071216220526
45468CB00002B/621